When Someone Dies

A Children's Mindful How-To Guide
On Grief and Loss

Andrea Dorn, MSW

Dedication

This book is dedicated to all children and grown-ups who have had to learn to live their lives without someone they love.

In loving memory of

Nicholas Fuss, Lloyd Fuss, Emil Helbling, and Gloria Beighley

When Someone Dies
Copyright © 2022 Andrea Dorn

Published by:
PESI Publishing
3839 White Ave
Eau Claire, WI 54703

Illustrations: Andrea Dorn
Cover: Andrea Dorn
Layout: Andrea Dorn & Amy Rubenzer

9781683734864 (print)
9781683734871 (ePUB)
9781683734888 (ePDF)
9781683734895 (KPF)

PESI Publishing
pesipublishing.com

🛑 STOP **Read Me First:** 🛑 STOP

Welcome to the Mindful Steps Series! The book you're about to read is called a "process story."

Process stories are incredible teaching tools that help caregivers and professionals:

- Share important, often abstract, concepts with children in a concrete way.

- Describe a new concept or skill to children while allowing them to process their feelings.

- Engage children in learning.

- Prompt important open-ended conversations with children to personalize the learning experience, build social-emotional skills, and strengthen connection and healthy attachment.

You can choose to read this book all the way through or just focus on the parts that are important to reiterate specifically with your child.

---

*Tip: This book is about more than just learning about bereavement. It's also about cultivating mindfulness, creating physical and emotional awareness, and practicing mindful language. To reinforce emotional intelligence and awareness, ask open-ended questions while reading each page. Use the suggested interactive prompts at the bottom of the pages (or create your own) to spark conversation. Depending on the age and development of your child, they may not always have the answers, but it will help them start thinking about the importance of these concepts. Because of the sensitivity of this topic, be sure to validate any thoughts or feelings that your child expresses.

Oh! Hi there! What is your name?

Really?! That is **MY** name too!

I am growing every day, and as I grow,
I get to learn lots of fun things!

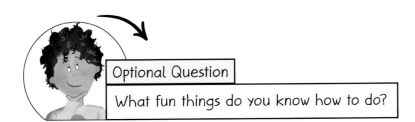

Optional Question

What fun things do you know how to do?

It can be exciting to learn new things
and to get to know new people in my life.

Optional Questions

What are some of your favorite things to do?
Who are some new people who have come into your life?

But sometimes people in my life go away.

People go away for different reasons and for different amounts of time. Sometimes, when someone goes away it means I can't see them right now, but I can see or talk to them again later.

Optional Question

Has there ever been a time when someone in your life went away, but then you got to see them again?

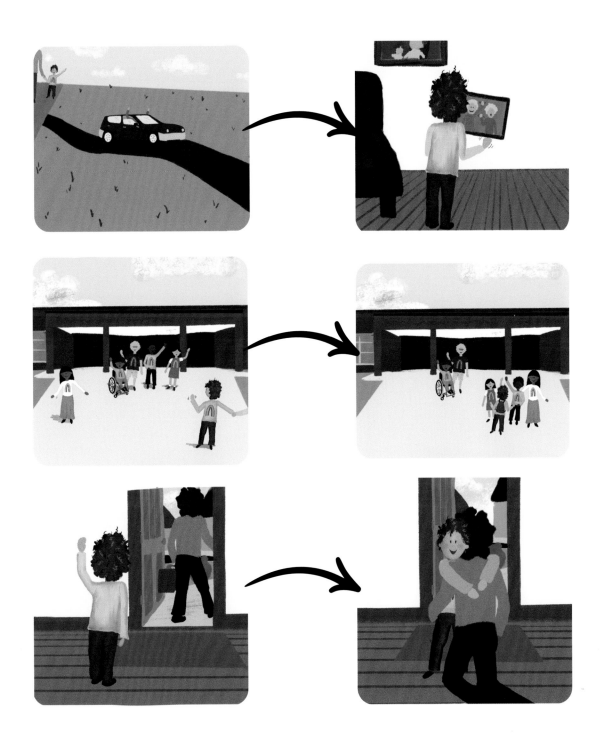

But there are times when people
go away because they have died.

When someone dies, it means that all the
parts of their body and mind have stopped working,
and they won't start working again. This means
I won't be able to see or talk to them anymore.

Optional Questions

Do you know anyone who has died?
Do you have any questions about what it means to die?

Dying is a normal part of life, but when someone close to me dies, lots of confusing things can happen inside of my body and around me.

To help me feel better,
I am learning how to say goodbye and grieve.

Optional Question

What do you think grief is?

Grief is a special word for all the feelings
I have when someone dies.

Grief feelings can be tricky, but learning how to work
through these feelings can help me feel better and
remember the person who died.

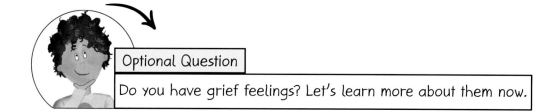

Optional Question

Do you have grief feelings? Let's learn more about them now.

Here is how I grieve and say
goodbye when someone dies.

When I first learn someone has died,
I might have a lot of different feelings.

I might feel mad. I might feel sad.
I might feel confused.
I might not know how to feel.
I might even feel just fine,
like nothing even happened!

It is good to know that any
feelings I have are okay.

After someone dies, it is very important to have special time to say goodbye.

Kids all over the world say goodbye to people who have died. They say goodbye in many different ways.

They may say goodbye. . .

At a funeral.

At a memorial service.

At a visitation.

By spreading ashes.

By visiting the gravesite
of the person who died.

By writing a letter or
drawing a goodbye picture.

Optional Questions

How and when did you get to say goodbye to the person who died? Who
said goodbye with you? If you haven't said goodbye yet, how would you like
to say goodbye?

After someone dies, there may be
some changes in my life.

The things around me might look or seem different.

People around me might also act or seem different.
They may have their own grief feelings.

Optional Questions

What is different in your life now? What looks the same?
Does anyone else in your life have their own grief feelings?

Over time, I might have lots of grief feelings inside of me. My grief feelings can be big or small.

Sometimes I might even have more than one feeling at a time.

And sometimes I might not even realize that my feelings are caused by my grief.

Here are some of the grief feelings I might have:

Sometimes I might feel very sad.

 Sometimes I might feel angry.

 Sometimes I might wonder if there's anything I can do to make the person who died come back.

 Sometimes I might forget that things have changed or that someone has died.

 And sometimes I might feel calm and peaceful or even happy when I remember the person who died.

Optional Questions

Do you feel any of these or any other feelings? Would you like to share how you're feeling right now? (See the expanded feelings chart near the back of this book for other common feelings associated with childhood bereavement.)

My grief feelings can show up at any time, for any reason,
and make me feel like I'm on a roller coaster.

They can take me up and down, last for a long time,
or change quickly.

They can be confusing and tiring.
But all of my feelings are okay and are
a normal part of grieving.

Optional Question

What has been the hardest part of having someone in your life die?

When I feel upset, there are three things I can do to help me feel better! I call these my "feel-better steps."

- **First,** I can stop and take a deep belly breath. I breathe in and let the air fill my belly like a balloon, then I breathe out and let my belly balloon deflate.

  I can notice how my body and heart feel and remember that it's okay to be upset. My feelings are important, and when I pay attention to them, they help me to know what I need!

- **Next,** I can feel my feet on the floor, spread my arms out wide, wrap them around myself in a big hug, and squeeze myself tight.

  I can remember that the feeling I'm having won't last forever.

- **Then,** I can find someone I love to talk to or sit with. I can remember I am never alone.

Optional Questions

What do you do when you're upset or sad? Whom can you talk to or sit with? Would you like to add any other feel-better steps?

Let's practice together:

I walk by a park and start to feel sad. Seeing the swings reminds me of the person in my life who died. What could I do?

1. Stop and breathe.

2. Give myself a hug.

3. Talk to someone I love.

That's it! Great job!

Let's try another one:

I wake up in the morning and don't feel happy.
I'm angry and annoyed by everyone,
and I don't even know why! What could I do?

1. Stop and breathe.

2. Give myself a hug.

3. Talk to someone I love.

You've got it—way to go!

Optional Question

When would be good times for you to use your feel-better steps? If you'd like, you can practice with those examples now. (Don't forget to include any other steps you came up with on your own!)

There are also some other things I can do to help me work through my grief feelings.

I can . . .

Draw a picture of how I feel.

Move my body.

Write a letter.

Allow myself to cry or feel my feelings.

Talk to a therapist or someone I trust.

Take care of myself.

Join a grief and loss group.

Sing or act out
my feelings.

Share memories of
the person who died
(it's okay if the memories are
good or not so good).

Optional Questions

Which ones have you tried? Which ones would you like to try?

My grief feelings will come and go and change over time. Sometimes I might forget to use my feel-better steps, or I might be too upset to work through my grief feelings.

That's okay. I can be gentle with myself and know I can keep practicing.

(And so can you!)

And when I'm ready, I can find new ways to remember or even feel close to the person who died.

I can . . .

Look for signs that remind me of them.

Start a journal of memories or make a memory box.

Look at pictures or videos.

Plant a tree.

Share stories.

Celebrate their birthday.

Start a tradition
in their honor.

Wear their favorite sweater, snuggle
up in their favorite blanket, or do
one of their favorite things.

Optional Question

Are there any other ways you could remember
or feel close to the person who died?

I might not feel this way right now, and it might not happen right away, but over time, and when I am ready, I will slowly start to feel better.

(And know that it's okay to feel better.)

I'll be able to remember the person who died and be happy at the same time.

And if the person who died was someone I loved very much, I'll know this person will always be a special part of my memories and the love we shared will always be a part of me.

Working through my grief feelings will help me grow and learn more than I ever knew was possible.

Optional Question

Would you like to share your favorite memory of the person in your life who died?

Sometimes growing up is fun, and sometimes
it can be tricky, but no matter what,
I'm glad I have YOU to grow with!

See you next time!

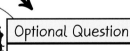

Optional Question

You are growing every day! What is one thing you can
name about yourself that you are proud of right now?

Meditation for Children

With one hand on my tummy and one hand on my chest,
I stop, breathe, and notice to give my mind some rest.

When someone dies, it's hard. Life changes day to day.
I'm learning things can change and that I can be okay.

Grief feelings can be tricky, for me and others too.
And when I feel upset, here is what I can do:

First, I stop and breathe. Then I give myself a hug.
Next, I sit or talk out loud with someone whom I love.

I listen to the birds that sing and see the sun
that shines. I'm grateful I was in your life
and you were part of mine.

Caregiver Mindfulness Exercise

It can be incredibly difficult to support a bereaved child, especially if you are struggling with the process of grief and loss yourself. I'd like to invite you to take a moment to care for yourself with a self-compassion exercise by Kristin Neff:

To begin this exercise, close your eyes, or pick a spot in the room to focus on, and soften your gaze. Take a few deep breaths, breathing in through your nose and out through your mouth. As you breathe, invite yourself to focus your attention on a mantra of self-compassion. This mantra is in the second person, but it is meant to be directed from yourself, toward yourself. Try your best to settle into the meaning and intention of these words:

This is a difficult time.
The emotions you're feeling make sense.
I am here for you.

Continue your slow and steady breathing, and repeat this mantra (or alter the phrasing in a way that feels best for you) out loud or in your mind. Repeat this as many times as you need.

Expanded Feelings Chart

 Acceptance: Sometimes I might feel calm and peaceful or even happy when thinking about the person who has died.

 Bargaining: I might wonder if there's anything I can do to make the person who died come back.

 Curious: Sometimes I might feel curious about what it means to die or what happened to the person who died.

 Denial: Sometimes I might forget that things have changed or that anyone has even gone away. I might even pretend that the person isn't gone.

 Distracted: Sometimes it might be hard to focus.

 Embarrassment: Sometimes I might feel embarrassed to talk about what happened, or I might feel embarrassed if people treat me differently than they used to.

 Fear: I might feel scared that someone else is going to die.

 Guilt: Sometimes I might feel like it was my fault that someone died, or I might feel guilty about having fun or being happy. I might feel guilty about not spending enough time with the person before they died. I might even feel guilty about making new relationships.

 Hopeful: Sometimes I might feel like things are going to be okay.

 Lonely: I might feel all alone or like no one understands what I am going through.

 Numb: Sometimes I might not know how to feel, or I might not feel anything at all.

 Physical sensations: Sometimes my body might hurt for no good reason.

 Worry: I might worry about other people when they have grief feelings. I might worry I will forget about the person who died.

Especially for Caregivers, Teachers, and Therapists

Dear Caregiver,

I'm so glad you have found your way to this book. Grief and bereavement become part of all of our lives at some point. They are not predictable, nor are they linear. They are difficult and complex topics, and when it comes to supporting ourselves and children, it is helpful to be equipped with as many resources as possible to work through this unpredictable process.

In navigating grief and loss, mindfulness, connection, and compassion are several important components to healing, but the ultimate goal is to learn how to build a new life in the wake of your loss. How can mindfulness play a supportive role in this process? In his book *Wherever You Go, There You Are*, Jon Kabat-Zinn defines mindfulness as "paying attention in a particular way: on purpose, in the present moment, and nonjudgmentally." Mindfulness is a practice that can help us be present with and experience the important emotions and feelings that accompany grief and bereavement. It can also help anchor and ground us in the present moment. This can inspire healing and facilitate connection with, and gratitude for, others and anything that comes our way.

This book is not an all-encompassing guide to bereavement but is intended to walk children through the loss and bereavement process in a simple and developmentally appropriate way. Embedded in this book are concepts developed by leading grief and loss experts, including Elisabeth Kübler-Ross, David Kessler, and J. W. Worden.

Read this book to your child as a way to encourage healthy expression of emotion and to normalize the feelings and uncertainty that come with the bereavement process. Though grief is an ongoing journey, I hope you find this guide to be a welcome and helpful tool on your path through this challenging time.

Warmest regards,

Andrea

Definitions

Grief:

The American Psychological Association defines grief as "the anguish experienced after significant loss, usually the death of a beloved person."

Defining grief for children:

In this book, grief is defined as "a special word for all the feelings I have when someone dies." Keeping the definition as simple as possible allows for a foundational understanding of this concept on which to grow.

Common types of grief:

Normal/uncomplicated grief: Normal grief consists of any feelings and behaviors that accompany a loss. These feelings typically last anywhere between 6 months and 2 years after a loss occurs, but normal grief can be shorter or longer depending on the nature of the loss.

Complicated grief: This is when grief becomes prolonged or traumatic.

Anticipatory grief: This type of grief occurs when an upcoming loss is expected or perceived. This can often manifest during cases of terminal illness or during situations where the outcome is unknown.

Disenfranchised grief: This refers to any grief that is not fully accepted or acknowledged by society. Examples include losing a pet, losing a belonging, moving, or losing a job.

Children's Understanding of Death

As children grow, their understanding of death changes over time.

Infants: Children this age are not able to conceptualize death, but they may respond to disruptions to routine, as well as to separation from, or emotional distance of, attachment figures.

Toddlers: Though toddlers have a greater understanding of relationships, and are able to recognize when someone is missing from their lives, they still are unable to conceptualize the finality of death. Children this age may become upset more easily, may be anxious or have separation anxiety, may become withdrawn, and may exhibit regression in previously learned skills.

Preschool: Children at this stage may have greater familiarity with the idea of death and dying, but they do not yet understand the concept of "forever." Preschool-aged children are similar to toddlers in their response to loss or disrupted routine, and they may respond with regressive behaviors that can seem unrelated to the loss.

School age: School-aged children are beginning to understand the finality of death. After age 8, children typically have a better understanding of mortality, so they may have increased curiosity about death and increased emotional reactions, including sadness, guilt, or anxiety. Loss that occurred at a younger age may be reprocessed during this time.

For more tips for helping kids work through grief, please visit www.andreadorn.com.